Elaine Reid

With best wishes,
Elaine Reid

Temenos 23

Temenos: a boundaried piece of ground
designated as a sacred space or sanctuary.

Created with support from The Barn, Aberdeenshire Council and Creative Scotland.

First published by The Curve of My Curiosity Press, 2018

Printed and bound by:
The Gatehouse Design and Print Agency,
Robert Gordon University, Aberdeen

ISBN: 978-1-5272-2098-0

A copy of this publication has been registered with the British Library.

www.elainereidwriting.co.uk

Contents

Meandering

Padding barefoot through summer's long grass,
perfumed by pine and honeysuckle,
dappled by beech and sorrowed by ash,
serenaded by the crank of the pheasant's call.

Perfumed by pine and honeysuckle,
collecting the counsel of holly and rowan,
serenaded by the crank of the pheasant's call,
shepherding time through my belonging.

Collecting the counsel of holly and rowan,
meandering through fireweed's wealth,
shepherding time through my belonging,
weaving the willow back into itself.

Meandering through fireweed's wealth,
dappled by beech and sorrowed by ash,
weaving the willow back into itself,
padding barefoot through summer's long grass.

Questions

I hang my questions in the rowan trees,
watch light glint through pinnate leaves
illuminating and dimming freely.

Letters drip golden to the ground below
trickling into passages, furrowed,
beginning the change I want to know.

My weekly weaving between silvered boughs
emboldens colour, lets perfumes arouse
fresh words to my page in the notes of my now.

I raise my eyes and smile at how
one word and a tree compose a vow
to the moment present: ripe, devout.

Shadows

shadows throw out
the shape of things
in dark simplicity

Answer

spring blossom flutters,
birds call and answer –
earth's trust holding on

Knowing

Your words chase mine around my head,
corralling them,
nosing my hand towards my pen,
neglected of late, avoided even,
because I know, within me, its reach -
trust its ability to write the deepest parts of me
in a three minute sprint across the page.
Freed from right or wrong
it hits the sweet spot -
that cluster of words that chime with the notes
of an untold story, a new wonder, a brainstorm not yet fully realised,
diving with the grace of beings that belong,
that slip smoothly in-between currents.

I wouldn't give it up for anything –
this ability to plunge.
But today, I am still not ready.

Together

We take our time
threading thoughts,
placing them particularly
so as not to impose
on the ends
of the others.

We gift one wonder at a time
into upturned palms
to roll around,
deciphering pleasures
before selecting another
in return.

We compose a sequence
then invite others
to trace the shapes
of our choosing,
loose and yielding,
sparkling with intent.

Entwined

For Mhairi

Your gentle kiss on my cheek on meeting,
the weightlessness of your fingertips

upon my arm, the fine-spun notes of your voice
cradling the air between us - such gestures

grace my life. The crispness of your attention,
the poised placement of your words

one in front of the other to reach your meaning
has moments arcing between us,

teasing out the patterns we have chanced
into something others can weave their own

narratives into. These sequences
mouthed, moved through - a kaleidoscope

of truths, mapping out discoveries
choreographing curiosity, stoked.

Imagine - This Wilderness

carTography

Honouring

gatherIng

elementS

Water's

wIsh

traveLling

amiDst

Earth's

encRiption

wiNd's

wEnding

fire'S

fecunditieS

Echoes

Sit with me in silence, writing,
    making the mark of your thoughts,
        collectively stating unique stories,
            emotions winding where they want.
Do not question flow's endeavour
    delving into mouldering depths,
        no bluff, no blush, no bolster,
            relax into the moments kept.
Intuition writes notes in the margins
    of answers already sensed,
        the pen providing a record
            of where your questions went.
Share the bones of what holds you,
    you to you and us to us,
        taking time, adventuring
            through every changing landscape lush
with joy and pain awaiting
    explorations risk,
        gift attention to the detail,
            do not let enquiry miss.
In this we honour all we are
    each to the other, reaching
        to place desires in harmony,
            to trust our tears to teaching.

Shelter

Shelter invites me under its branches and leaves,
growing a space for me
to tell my stories, when ready.

Belong

(to the labyrinth)

I belong in the darkness now
as I circumambulate history's coils,
walking to answers echoed through time
inheriting question's unravelling spoils.

Behold (The Other Side)

There was one duckling I watched
and two moles I found
and at least three pigeons whose feathers I discovered
blood-smucked
with some other animal's saliva
holding their weight to the ground.

My breath snagged on every occasion,
my brain wheeling through the telling tales of
a duckling not following its mother,
a mole sunbathing, tummy up,
torn feathers clumped and scattered around.

I tried to make my eyes look -
the way I would at a duck landing on water,
its out-stretched wings back-lit by the sun.

My living louder,
my wish to witness beating hard
to lift itself into the wind.

Whisper

Whisper waits
well back from the path
for senses to be pricked,
                          enough

to pick it up.

Enough

A butterfly lands from the sky -
a peacock, startling me
parading its wings across my page.

I note its four eyespots:
two amethyst, two amber,
and ten white dots elsewhere, smudged.

The plumpness of its suede-brown body
tempts me, almost, to touch.
Its two slender antennae quiver in the breeze.

It stays for a second more,
and another,
then lifts and leaves.

Later, I wonder
what did it take away of me,
of us?

Some Times

Spring

the blonde grass
in the field beyond -
a beach to the sea of the sky

the warmed earth
embraces the arch of each foot,
welcomes them home

a half-moon slotted
in the afternoon sky,
ready and waiting

Autumn

the sawing of logs
flutes the air
left silent by nature's toil

the songs of the leaves
crescendoing
in autumn's rivers of wind

browned cow parsley
still erect
paying the wind with its seeds

red crocosmia tongues,
self-seeded through mint
making themselves heard

Breathe – Warm Up 23

I focus my mind inward and breathe

to trace the arc of my gut in darkness,
the concave reflex of the shoulders of shelter,
the circling of the lips to push out a whisper,
the contraction in the throat of shadow,

the bow of the temples to instinct's knowing,
the twisting of the limbs of entwine,
the thrashing about of the bones of the wild,
the restack in the spine of unfurl,

the release of squeezed muscles found in forget,
the raise of the eyes in dream,
the tilt of the head to direct the question,
the tip-toe teetering of feet on the edge,

the extension of hands in our coming together,
the rise of the sternum when told to Behold!,
the flourish in the wrist that invites imagine,
the scooping of palms to remember,

the reverberation in the ribcage of echoes,
the pulse of the core in the blood of enough,
the slowing down of each step of meander,
the sideways sway in the knees of sometimes,

and that tingle in fingertips finding the answer,
with the flow in and out of the skin of belong.

Remember

chalk white vapour trail
smudging, fading
in summer's stretched out seconds

Wild

Wild reclines
astride the fork
of abandonment and need,
greedy
pronouncing itself
on the push and the pull
of my lips, my tongue, my teeth –
the ignition of why in its dotted eye,
splaying.

Darkness

Darkness hangs
hidden amongst spent branches,
brittle now,
abandoned by growth.

Unfurl

Telling is tucked,
keeping its sentences
furled, for now.

The words, waiting
to be unwound
from silence.

Each tongue
a scroll
of its body of knowing.

41

Dream

Just get going. And never submit.
Consider doubt, yes, but don't give in to it.
Exhilarate. Enliven. In your entirety.

Remember the sunrise of you in your boots
determined to answer, to flourish, to scoop.
Fresh. Flouncy. Free.

I'm done at last with the road to *Why?*
Give me open fields, forests, hillsides,
abandon *Should* and *Must* to the sea.

Watch out for sign posts, harvest attention,
relish the running of your fingers into things.
Wait. Witness. Be.

Let the recipes of destiny's mishaps
make fragrant flowers from the tongues of perhaps.
Perfume. Promise. Possibility.

Forget

Relax back into forgetting,
      releasing your head to my shoulder,
            sheltering tenderness under my own,
                  the moment lit, reflected.

You turn and offer me your arms,
      gathering me from my precipice,
            curiousness spread wide as wings,
                  feathering in to darkness.

Our bodies fold into shadow,
      sweeping it through with our fingertips,
            coming to stillness, mirroring,
                  the breathing of beacons alight.

Edge

It's human nature to claim a space
boundaried by stone pledged
to the purpose of holding firm -
cold granite fragments fitted together
to keep us from the chaos of the unknown.
And inside these dykes we'll prune and we'll weed
and we'll pollard until we get
what we think we want from the soil beneath us,
digging in to nature's undulations
and calling it Design. But outside,
the brambles still snake into spaces,
roses strike out, roots unearth themselves,
sticky willy entangles its neighbours still,
and underground, the willow herb
continues to colonise, popping up brightly
in its own arrangements of fiery pleasure.

Acknowledgements

I would like to thank The Barn and in particular, Linzy McAvoy for entrusting me with the Flourish wellbeing project and for the opportunity to write and work within the sanctuary of the Wild Garden. I would like to express my gratitude to Aberdeenshire Council and Creative Scotland for their support via the VACMA award, and to Shane Strachan and the Aberdeen Writers' Studio for their invaluable support and feedback on specific poems. Thanks also to choreographer, Mhairi Allan for inspiring me and helping me to unfurl my practice further.

With special thanks to my husband, Eric for his unfailing support in all my creative endeavours and to Jenna and Callum for making life so rich and so treasured. To Ruth and Michael, thank you for holding my hand, always. And finally, with love to Mum.

Temenos 23 grew out of Elaine Reid's year as Writer in Residence at The Barn, Banchory. Based in the Wild Garden she led the Flourish programme which emphasised the wellbeing benefits of writing in nature. She created a word installation for the project launch which included 23 acrylic words hung in the trees, captured here in her photographs. These became the focus for her writing workshops for schools and the wider community. *Breathe*, a collaboration between Elaine and choreographer, Mhairi Allan also used these words as inspiration for a series of found poetry and movement workshops. The poems gathered here reflect on all those experiences and have been organised as you would find the words walking round the garden clockwise. Themes such as nature's cycles and its wildness, our human capacity for self-knowing and connection, as well as the process of therapeutic writing itself are explored.

Elaine Reid was born in Aberdeen. She is a writer and an artist with a background in counselling and has been facilitating Words for Wellbeing workshops since 2010.

Cover image:
The Wild Garden,
The Barn, Banchory.

Price £10

ISBN 978-1-5272-2098-0

9 781527 220980